YOU CAN BEGIN AGAIN

By
Dr. Gerald Mann

 **GERALD MANN MINISTRIES**
P.O. BOX 160100
AUSTIN, TX 78716
(800) 974-HOPE (4673)

You Can Begin Again
ISBN 0-9678502-1-5

This book, or parts thereof, may not be reproduced in any form without written permission of Gerald Mann Ministries.

Unless otherwise noted, all Scripture references are from the Good News Bible, Today's English Version, Second Edition © 1992, Thomas Nelson Publishers, Nashville, TN.

Scripture references marked KJV are from the King James Version of the Bible.

Names are changed on all personal references used in examples unless otherwise noted.

TABLE OF CONTENTS

Introduction		9
1	You Can Begin Again After You Have Been Left Out	11
2	You Can Begin Again After Great Sorrow	25
3	You Can Begin Again After Moral Failure	39
4	You Can Begin Again After 40	51
5	You Can Begin Again After Burnout	65
6	You Can Begin Again After Betrayal	75
About The Author		87

"God puts people right through their faith in Jesus Christ. God does this to all who believe in Christ, because there is no difference at all: everyone has sinned and is far away from God's saving presence. But by the free gift of God's grace all are put right with him through Christ Jesus who sets them free."

Romans 3:22-24

INTRODUCTION

You can begin again!

In this book, I deal with six common life crises and show you how you can start over—after you've been left out, after great sorrow, after moral failure, after 40, after burnout, and after betrayal.

The methods I will share with you are drawn straight from Biblical example. The Bible is where I turn in times of trial, because it offers hope for a new beginning. Its recurrent theme is that we should not give up on ourselves because with the grace of God, we can become a new creation in Jesus Christ. No matter what sorrows we suffer, what losses we experience, or what pains we endure—we do not have to be limited or held back by our failures, our hurts, or even our age. No matter what we have done, no matter where we have been, through God's gracc, we all can begin again!

Gerald Mann

CHAPTER ONE

YOU CAN BEGIN AGAIN... AFTER YOU HAVE BEEN LEFT OUT

...AFTER YOU HAVE BEEN LEFT OUT

Everyone feels left out at some point in his or her life. Whether it is as minor as not being selected for the baseball team at school, or as devastating as being left by a spouse, you can begin again after being left out. The secrets to starting over are found in Psalm 23—a passage often used at funerals—but I believe it is really a commencement Psalm that shows us how to begin again after we have been left out. David said:

> *The L<small>ORD</small> is my shepherd;*
> *I have everything I need.*
> *He lets me rest in fields of green*
> *grass*
> *and leads me to quiet pools of*
> *fresh water.*
> *He gives me new strength.*
> *He guides me in the right paths,*
> *as he has promised.*
> *Even if I go through the deepest*
> *darkness,*
> *I will not be afraid, L<small>ORD</small>,*
> *for you are with me.*

> *Your shepherd's rod and staff*
> *protect me.*
>
> *You prepare a banquet for me,*
> *where all my enemies can*
> *see me;*
> *you welcome me as an honored*
> *guest*
> *and fill my cup to the brim.*
> *I know that your goodness and*
> *love will be with me all my*
> *life;*
> *and your house will be my home*
> *as long as I live. (Psalm 23:1-6)*

This Psalm shows how to begin again, even after you have been left out.

The need to be included and have a place to belong is one of our most basic needs. I was seven years old, and my brother was eleven when one night, while I was supposed to be sleeping, I overheard my parents talking in the next room. I will never forget hearing my father say, "I have this wonderful fishing trip planned, but we need to figure out a way for me to take Wayne and leave little Jerry at home."

Although this happened over 57 years ago, I remember those words as though they were spoken yesterday. I am sure you can identify with how I felt, as everyone has had the experience of being left out.

No one ever felt more left out than King David. You will remember that God told the Prophet Samuel to go to Bethlehem to the house of Jesse. Jesse had several sons, one of whom was to become the future King of Israel. God instructed Samuel to look at them, at which time He would reveal the chosen one.

When Samuel arrived at Jesse's house, he said, "Bring me your sons," so Jesse presented his sons. The first one was tall and handsome—with even, white teeth and sparkling eyes—but he was not the right one, so Jesse brought forth six more sons, one by one.

Then Samuel asked Jesse, "Do you have any other sons?"

"Oh yes, there's one more—David—but he is only a shepherd." A shepherd was the lowest rung of Hebrew society. David lived with the sheep, smelled like them, and spent his time fending off bears and lions with rocks and clubs. There was not much hope for him. He was considered the loser of the family.

However, as we now know, David eventually became the greatest king in the history of Israel. How did he overcome rejection to achieve his destiny? How did he begin again after he felt left out?

I believe Psalm 23 gives us the answer in the first verse: *"The LORD is my shepherd; I have everything I need."* In the desert, David was forced to depend on God to be his Shepherd. The **desert** where David spent his time with the sheep, actually became his **dessert**. If you have felt rejected, you will not be left out forever if you allow the Lord to become your Shepherd and meet your needs.

A leading psychoanalyst named Alfred Adler studied well-adjusted people to formulate his ideas about what makes people emotionally healthy. He discovered that everyone has five basic needs that need to be fulfilled: physiological needs, the need for safety, the need to belong, the need for self-esteem, and the necessity of having a dream. We find these all represented in Psalm 23.

1. Let the Lord provide for your physiological needs. If a man is hungry, without food, nourishment, rest, and replenishment, his attention and concentration are focused on survival. His basic, physiological needs must first be met before he can consider anything else.

Listen to what David says: *"He lets me rest in fields of green grass and leads me to quiet pools of fresh water. He gives me new strength."* David learned in the desert to depend on God and let Him be Shepherd of his physiological needs, and God never failed to provide.

America has become a nation obsessed with accumulating material possessions because we have neglected the simple truth that the Lord is our Shepherd. My challenge to you is to trust in God, and let Him be the Shepherd of your physiological needs. This does not mean taking on a new regimen in life, rather it means adopting a new rhythm in life. Whenever you are worried about making ends meet, providing food, or acquiring clothing, remember: *"The LORD is my shepherd; I have everything I need."*

If you learn to depend on God for your physiological needs, you can begin again after you have been left out. Have faith in God; get a new rhythm in your life.

2. Let the Lord be the Shepherd of your safety. David says, *"He guides me in the right paths, as he has promised. Even if I go through the deepest darkness, I will not be afraid, LORD, for you are with me. Your shepherd's rod and staff protect me."*

The safe paths are the ones on which you will neither slip, nor fall. If you have ever been to the Judean Hills in Southern Israel, you know that Death Valley is a deep gorge that runs through the hills down to Jericho. It is always in the shadows, and lions and bears lurk there. Yet David said, *"Even if I go through the deepest darkness, I will not be afraid..."*

Safety needs must be met; people cannot function properly when living in fear. We need a pathway in life that is dependable and safe, so that we may walk in confidence. If the Lord is the Shepherd of our safety, we have no need for fear. No matter how well we take care of ourselves, we are mortal beings. There can be no peace of mind, no way to overcome feeling mortal, except to depend upon God and His rod and staff.

3. Let the Lord be the Shepherd of your need to belong. After we have had our physiological and safety needs met, we all need a sense of community—a place to belong and be loved.

True love is belonging, and it is found only in stable environments. That is why families are so important and why divorce can be so destructive to a child's nature.

Robert Frost defined the family as "a place where you go and they have to take you in." That is what has built our church family at Riverbend Church where I pastor. It doesn't matter who people are, how bad they have been, or what they have done, the door is always open, and we take them in. I look across our congregation every week, and I see people who had no place else to go. Our church is filled with outcasts who needed to be taken in.

People cannot love you perfectly. Only God can do that, so let the Lord be the Shepherd of your love needs and provide you with a place to belong.

4. Let the Lord be the Shepherd of your need for esteem. After our physiological and safety needs and the necessity of belonging, we have a need for self-respect. One of the things I learned about many inmates in prison is that they do not know how to achieve anything, and as a result, they lack self-respect. We all need to be able to do something for which we can respect ourselves. We need to be proud of what we do.

Listen to David's words: *"You prepare a banquet for me, where all my enemies can see me; you welcome me as an honored guest and fill my cup to the brim."* Having a full cup was a symbol of being highly respected and esteemed. David knew that no matter what happened, God valued him.

When David was only 16 years old, he saw the giant Goliath threatening God's people and decided he could kill him. Highly doubtful, people asked David, "with what?" David simply replied, "with my sling-shot."

There was Goliath, in his armor with all of Israel cowering in fear before him, and young David claiming he could defeat him. David had absolutely no doubt that he could do it because he had developed his skills by conquering the lion and bear. God was the Shepherd of David's esteem.

5. Let the Lord be the Shepherd of your dreams. David said, *"I know that your goodness and love will be with me all my life; and your house will be my home as long as I live."* David was attaching his dreams to God's dreams, when he said that God's house would be his home for the rest of his life.

God did not create us for mediocrity. He continually calls us to greatness. Do you have a dream big enough for God to be part of it? What is your dream? How big is it? What do you want to do with your life? Can you hitch your dream to God's dream, like David did?

Let's consider for a moment the life and dreams of one man. In 1832, this man lost his job and was defeated in a race for the legislature.

YOU CAN BEGIN AGAIN

In 1833, he failed in business and went broke. He did win the election to the legislature in 1834, but his victory was saddened by the death of his sweetheart in 1835. In 1836, he had a nervous breakdown. He was defeated for Speaker of the House in 1838, and five years later in 1843, he was defeated for a seat in Congress. He was finally elected to Congress in 1846, but lost his reelection campaign in 1848. A year later, he was rejected for Land Officer, and in 1855 he lost a bid for the U.S. Senate. He lost the nomination for vice presidency of the United States in 1856, and three years later was again defeated for the Senate. Even with so many setbacks, disappointments, and crushing defeats, he did not quit. He held on to his dreams and in 1860, Abraham Lincoln became President of the United States of America in one of this nation's darkest hours.

Just before his death, President Lincoln said, "God selects His own instruments and sometimes He selects real strange ones. For instance, He chose me to steer the ship through a great crisis."

No matter how many times you are rejected,

you can begin again if you trust in the Lord to be your Shepherd and provide for all of your needs.

CHAPTER TWO

YOU CAN BEGIN AGAIN... AFTER GREAT SORROW

No matter how much we try to shelter or protect ourselves, at some point or another, we all will experience great sorrow. But if we follow King David's example, we can move through the pain to begin again. One of the greatest losses in King David's life is described in 2 Samuel, Chapter 12. After his sin with Bathsheba:

The LORD caused the child that Uriah's wife had borne to David to become very sick. David prayed to God that the child would get well. He refused to eat anything, and every night he went into his room and spent the night lying on the floor. His court officials went to him and tried to make him get up, but he refused and would not eat anything with them. A week later the child died, and David's officials were afraid to tell him the news. They said, "While the child was living, David wouldn't answer us when we spoke to him. How can we tell him that his child is dead? He might do himself some harm!"

When David noticed them whispering to each other, he realized that the child had died. So he asked them, "Is the child dead?"

"Yes, he is," they answered.

David got up from the floor, took a bath, combed his hair, and changed his clothes. Then he went and worshipped in the house of the LORD. When he returned to the palace, he asked for food and ate it as soon as it was served. "We don't understand this," his officials said to him. "While the child was alive, you wept for him and would not eat; but as soon as he died, you got up and ate!"

"Yes," David answered, "I did fast and weep while he was still alive. I thought that the LORD might be merciful to me and not let the child die. But now that he is dead, why should I fast? Could I bring the child back to life? I will someday go to where he is, but he can never come back to me." (2 Samuel 12:15-23)

When I began preparing this series on *"You Can Begin Again,"* I had no idea that I was on the threshold of the greatest loss of my life. My precious wife of almost 42 years went to be with the Lord.

With Lois gone just a few weeks before our 42nd anniversary, I wish I could tell you that I received some great visitation from God, or that I had comforting dreams or visions of my wife, but that did not happen. I wish I could tell you that I experienced great victories over my suffering, but that simply was not the way it was.

There are many types of grief. Your grief may be like mine—the loss of a loved one. You may have lost your marriage or your health. Perhaps you lost a big business deal or a treasured relationship with someone you loved. There are all kinds of grief, and what I am going to share with you for dealing with it is not "psychotherapy from Dr. Gerald Mann." This is coming from someone who has experienced intense sorrow. I want to simply share with you four things that are helping me get through the greatest loss of my life.

YOU CAN BEGIN AGAIN

1. Good memories. After my wife's death, my first reaction was guilt and self-incrimination. I thought of all the times I was not present with her. I felt I had not been the husband I should have been, or the helper I could have been when she was sick. But then, one thought played over and over deep in my mind. I believe God planted it there. A voice said to me, "you must have loved her very much, because nobody could feel that guilty unless they cared deeply." That gave me the little boost I needed to get through a very dark day.

When we experience a great loss, our mind often haunts us by bringing up bad memories. So, in the midst of my loss I am trying to hold on to the multitude of good memories that Lois and I shared. These memories are not the greatest, or most significant events of our lives, but the little things—like having coffee together once a day and having our TAD—our "talk a day," as we called it. These are the small, but precious memories I hold on to that help me see beyond my grief.

Willie Nelson, my good friend of 30 years, has

a song, which says, "Remember the good times. They are fewer in number and easier to recall." Don't spend too much time on the bad times. Their staggering numbers are overwhelming.

You can begin again after great sorrow—no matter what your loss. Everyone will experience great loss at some time in his or her life, and when it happens, I encourage you to recall the good memories.

2. Gracious people. Every time I started complaining to God about losing the love of my life, He would not answer me. Instead, He would send some gracious friend to comfort me. I could not even keep up with reading all of the letters and cards from my own church congregation. It started with 200, and every day, the stack grew higher. Thousands of people wrote and did so many gracious things for me. I am convinced that God does not show Himself in the world because He expects us to do that.

Before this experience, I had never felt like a "beloved" pastor. I felt like I was a good leader who worked hard and dreamed great dreams, but I never felt very loved. Now, I no longer feel that way. I have never before felt as safe with who I am and where I am, and it is because of the gracious people around me.

Someone asked me recently, "If you were going to use an analogy to describe your church, which one best fits?" It is not an organization, nor is it a cause. The best model I can come up with is a hospital. My church is a place for hurting people to come and be healed.

Healing has come to me during my hard time through gracious people. When your suffering comes, hang on to such people. You can begin again, even in the depths of despair if you will allow yourself to be surrounded and healed by gracious people.

3. Glad reunions. Lois' death triggered many reunions with people I had neither seen, nor heard from in years. There were glad reunions with old friends and even some foes, as they all rallied to my side. One of my former rivals, upon hearing of my wife's death, came to comfort me and is now a friend. He probably always was, and I was just unable to recognize it.

My sister and I had not spoken to each other

for four years. You would not expect that from someone who is a preacher, would you? We were estranged all those years, but after my wife's death, she showed up unannounced, and we reconciled.

As a young boy, I lived in a small town of 2,000 people. There was a boy named Danny, who was recognized as the greatest football star in the community. When my family moved to town, we became competitors. I had not heard from him in years, but after Lois died, I received a letter from him, in which he wrote:

> I always thought the best of Lois. She was always so glad to see everyone. She was fun to be around. I can remember her laughter...we will all miss her. Jerry, at our last reunion you made apologies for your behavior in high school. After thinking about it, we all said and did things we wish we could retract. We all have apologies to make, but you are the only one who did. To say that I was surprised when you entered

the ministry would be an understatement, but you showed us all that you were for real. I, for one, am proud of your success and glad to have been your classmate and your teammate. I shall always remember Lois on the sidelines, cheering for you. I am certain she still is and always will be.

You can begin again if you will let your pain trigger glad reunions with people who can enrich your life. Hang on to glad reunions.

4. God's future. God's future is what I am holding on to the most in my own time of grief. Every time I wanted to quit after Lois' death, God imposed His future on me. We have a 13 year-old grandchild who lives at our house, and even though I am 62 years old, I can't think about quitting or giving up because she is the future, as are my beautiful children.

When King David experienced the loss of his child, he grieved *before* his son died, not afterwards. I believe he actually had things in the proper focus. He explained, *"I will some day go to where he is, but he can never come back to me."* David understood that there is only one option after a great loss and that is to move forward. That does not mean that we forget our loss, it just means that our grieving does not entrap or immobilize us.

I certainly wanted to give up and quit after my wife's death, but God kept imposing His future on me. Forward is the only direction I can go. All the great plans Lois and I made for our "golden years" are gone. The future we planned together no longer exists. The only future I have now is God's future.

I have come to know in a way that I never knew before the truth of the Apostle Paul's message to the Corinthians. He wrote, *"...we shall not all die, but when the last trumpet sounds, we shall all be changed in an instant, as quickly as the blinking of an eye. For when the trumpet sounds, the dead will be raised, never to die again..." (1 Corinthians 15:51-52)*

We must concentrate on making plans and executing them, doing our very best, but never forgetting that when the darkness of grief comes, we always have God's future. Forward is the only direction to go.

I had a dear friend, John Claypool, who lost his daughter, Laura, to leukemia when she was only 13 years old. Twelve years later while he was speaking at a conference, a woman asked if she could share something with him. She told him about a dream she had had, in which she was at Oxford University Library. In the dream, she saw a young woman in her 20's, with beautiful blonde hair, sitting at a table. The young woman motioned for the lady to come and sit down by her, and she said, "I'm Doctor Claypool. I think you know my father."

"I don't know him," the woman answered, "but I have heard him speak a few times."

The young woman said, "My colleagues and I are working on a cure for leukemia, and every time we think we have the problem solved, it evaporates in our hands. We get so close, but we don't solve it. I've become convinced in recent days that it is because my father will not let me go. If you see my father please tell him to let me go and live my life, so that he can live his."

The first time I heard that story, it sounded a bit cruel. Now I know its truth. If you are experiencing a great loss—or when you do experience one in the future—you have no other option but to go forward, and that is done by holding on to good memories, surrounding yourself with gracious people, experiencing glad reunions, and accepting God's future for you.

CHAPTER THREE

YOU CAN BEGIN AGAIN... AFTER MORAL FAILURE

You can begin again—even after moral failure. You will recall that God promoted King David to great heights of success, then he had an affair with Bathsheba, and upon finding she was pregnant, he had her husband murdered. When the Prophet Nathan exposed David's sin, many thought it would be the end of him, but it wasn't. David's new beginning is found in Psalm 51.

Be merciful to me, O God,
> *because of your constant love.*
Because of your great mercy
> *wipe away my sins!*
Wash away all my evil
> *and make me clean from my sin!*

I recognize my faults;
> *I am always conscious of my sins.*
I have sinned against you—only
>> *against you—*
> *and done what you consider evil.*
So you are right in judging me;
> *you are justified in condemning me.*
I have been evil from the day I was born;

> *from the time I was conceived, I*
> *have been sinful.*

> *Sincerity and truth are what you require;*
> *fill my mind with your wisdom.*
> *Remove my sin, and I will be clean;*
> *wash me, and I will be whiter*
> *than snow.*
> *Let me hear the sounds of joy and*
> *gladness;*
> *and though you have crushed me*
> *and broken me,*
> *I will be happy once again.*
> *Close your eyes to my sins*
> *and wipe out all my evil.*

> *Create a pure heart in me, O God,*
> *and put a new and loyal spirit in me.*
> *Do not banish me from your presence;*
> *do not take your holy spirit away*
> *from me.*
> *Give me again the joy that comes*
> *from your salvation,*
> *and make me willing to obey you.*

Then I will teach sinners your commands,
  and they will turn back to you.

Spare my life, O God, and save me,
  and I will gladly proclaim your
    righteousness.
Help me to speak, Lord,
  and I will praise you.

You do not want sacrifices,
  or I would offer them;
you are not pleased with burnt
    offerings.
My sacrifice is a humble spirit,
    O God;
  you will not reject a humble
    and repentant heart.
  (Psalm 51:1-17)

I had a brilliant classmate at seminary who made good grades, was a wonderful speaker, and became the pastor of a great church. He rose to the top of his denomination, and probably would have eventually become the youngest president in the history of the Southern Baptist Convention. Then, he had an extra-marital affair, and his world came crashing down around him. He resigned amidst scandal and disgrace.

When I heard about it, I wrote him a note telling him, "Regardless of what you have done or ever will do, I am your friend, and I wish the best for you." About two years later I saw this man in an airport. He came running over, hugged me, and told me that of all the ministers he knew, I was the only one who wrote him a letter of encouragement.

We went to have coffee together, and I asked him, "Tell me how you ended up having an affair and losing your character."

"You have it backwards," he said. "I didn't have an affair and lose my character. I lost my character, and then I had an affair."

When he said that, I thought to myself, "That's just like David's story. He didn't have an affair and lose his character. He lost his character and then had an affair." Immorality is failing to live up to what we can be. It is not breaking rules. It is failing to match what we were created to be. Moral failure is breaking relationships.

When David was anointed to be king, the Bible says he had the Spirit of God—in Hebrew this means "the wind of God." Later on, when he failed to go to war and do what he was supposed to do, the "wind" of God's power left him. He lost the wind in his sails.

Some people say that David never recovered from his moral disgrace, but I do not believe that. David had a son named Solomon, who was the wisest man who ever lived. Where did Solomon get his wisdom? He got much of it by sitting at the feet of a broken, battle-scarred warrior named David.

How did David recover from his great moral disgrace? How do we begin again after moral failure? Psalm 51 contains the clues. David confessed three things:

1. David confessed what really went wrong. He said, *"I have sinned against you—only against you..."* We might be inclined to believe he had sinned against Bathsheba, her husband, Uriah, who was murdered, or the nation he led as king. But David said that it was

God alone against whom he had sinned. He was admitting what really went wrong, and that was the fact that he had left God out of the equation of his life. Sins are the things we do when we leave God out of the equation of our lives. Secular humanism is nothing more than living life without reference to God. Instead of keeping God at the hub of things, we move Him to the periphery of our lives.

David did not have a mid-life crisis; he had a theological problem. David put God on the periphery of his life. To begin again after moral failure, we must own up to what really went wrong, and return the center point of our lives back to God.

2. David confessed what he really needed. In Psalm 51:6-15, David asks for wisdom, sincerity, joy, a pure heart, and a loyal spirit.

When I was growing up, one of my spiritual mentors was an African-American preacher, named Pastor Diggs. Pastor Diggs had a little one-room church that had existed since the time of slavery. He had about 50 people in his congregation. I would sometimes help him clean up around the church and mow the grass, so he would let me sit in the doorway and listen while they held church services. In my short pants and bare-feet, I would sit in the entryway to listen to Pastor Diggs. Every time he spoke about David and Psalm 51, he would say, "David knew what he needed. He didn't need a wax job. He didn't need polish or refinement. He needed an overhaul!" That is what we really need when we have experienced moral failure.

I received a letter from a woman who told me that her father had been the head deacon in their church when she was a child. He had served on the school board and had been a civic leader in the community. When she was 12 years old, her father began to sexually molest her. At the age of 16, she ran away from home and got into drugs and alcohol, had multiple marriages, and always shunned her family. She was considered the "black sheep" of the family, and she never told her mother or brothers what her father had done to her. When her father was diagnosed with terminal cancer, her family begged her to come home and reconcile with him.

She arrived home to find her father wasted away to less than 100 pounds. She wrote, "I went into his room with every intention of saying, 'You have created a cancer in my soul that has eaten at me all these years, and you deserve what you get.' But in a whisper he asked me, 'Can you ever forgive me for what I have done?'"

That young woman turned and walked out of that room without a word. When she was alone, she began to weep and said, "Oh God, forgive me. I cannot forgive him." She wrote, "Dr. Mann, something miraculous happened at that moment. All of my hatred and bitterness disappeared." What this young woman needed was a whole new set of working parts that only God could give her.

If you are to begin again after moral failure, you must own up to what you really need—and that is something you cannot get for yourself. David asked for sincerity, loyalty, cleansing, a new spirit, and a new heart. He understood that he did not need to refine his outward character; he needed a whole new set of insides.

3. David confessed the only thing he could

really do. He told God, "I would offer sacrifices and offerings, but they would do no good." He said, "I cannot work my way out of what I did. It is done. I cannot redo it. I cannot work harder to try to fix it. All I have to rely on is Your grace. Only a broken heart and humble spirit will do any good."

David did the only thing he could really do—he relied upon the grace of God and surrendered himself to Him. He asked God to, "do for me what I cannot do for myself."

I have a subtle pride about me—and maybe you do too—which makes me think that when I do something wrong, I can repair or mend it. Of course, I can keep the rules better or make amends, but the reality is that the only thing anyone has to rely upon is the grace of God.

Gordon McDonald, who built a great church in Massachusetts, had an adulterous affair at the pinnacle of his career. He confessed to his wife and his church, resigned, and submitted himself to spiritual counsel and restoration. Five years later, he returned to pastor that church as a new person. He later wrote a book entitled,

"Rebuilding Our Broken World," in which he said that at the depths of his despair, he realized there was nothing he could do to atone for what he had done. It was already done, and he could not fix it. He said that for the first time, he discovered the grace of God. The grace of God means that He is the only one left who will provide a tomorrow.

Since my wife died, God's grace for me has come to mean "guts"—or courage. I have even found an acronym for "guts." **G** means gladness—reminiscing about the joys I shared with her. **U** means understanding—God understands my pain and anger. **T** means tomorrow—life must go on. **S** means sanity.

What do you do when you fail morally? Own up to what really went wrong—a broken relationship with God. Confess what is really needed, which is not a little polish on the outside, but a whole new set of inner workings. Own up to the only thing to be done—surrender yourself to God's grace. You cannot do it alone. He can. Just let Him.

CHAPTER FOUR

YOU CAN BEGIN AGAIN... AFTER 40

There was an elderly man who celebrated his 97th birthday, and someone asked him what it was like to be that old. He said, "Well I can only see about 10 yards. I don't hear very well anymore, my hands are arthritic, and I can only lift my right foot up by grabbing it with both hands. But thank God, I can still drive!"

Every time I think about getting older, I remember that story. When we speak of old age, more often than not, we treat it humorously. To say someone is "old" is now considered to be politically incorrect. We are supposed to use words like "aging, maturing, or entering the golden years." In all the advertisements on the television and radio, or in print, "new" is a synonym for good. "Old," however, implies "bad." These ads continually tell us, "you don't want the old product; you *need* the new one." America is the only country in the world that as a culture, not only ignores the wisdom of elders, but abhors it. We have become obsessed with youth and terrified of mortality. We retreat from the whole concept of aging.

We are all programmed early in life to be

plagued by what I call "the three dogs of despair," that hound us as we get older. The first of these is the feeling of worthlessness, that a person has a lesser value because of his or her age—like an automobile, the older it is the less it is worth. The second is the feeling of failure. Perhaps a person never lived up to his dreams or potential, and as a consequence feels like a failure. The third is feeling obsolete, the idea of being washed up. Do you know where the phrase "washed up" originally came from? It came from things that died in the ocean and were washed up on the beach! We all have these three feelings, they have been programmed into us by society and the media.

Psalm 139 is a psalm written in David's old age. Even after his great moral failure, David came back and lived to a ripe old age. He had a life full of honors, riches, and truth. I believe that this psalm shows us how David dealt with these "dogs of despair" as he aged.

1. Feelings of worthlessness. How did David deal with feeling that he was of no value because he was old? Psalm 139 shows us that he came to understand that God was a God of grace and forgiveness. David said:

> *LORD, you have examined me*
> *and you know me.*
> *You know everything I do;*
> *from far away you understand*
> *all my thoughts.*
> *You see me, whether I am*
> *working or resting;*
> *you know all my actions.*
> *Even before I speak,*
> *you already know what I*
> *will say.*
> *You are all around me on every*
> *side;*
> *you protect me with your power.*
> *(Psalm 139:1-5)*

As a Baptist, I grew up knowing what grace was intellectually, but I never internalized it in my heart. I was in the ministry for over 20 years before I understood the incomprehensible grace of God. He knows everything there is to know about me—not just the good things—but also all of the junk and garbage. Yet, He continues to surround me with His love and forgiveness.

There is no way to overcome feelings of worthlessness unless we can get in touch with how God feels about us. We must come to love ourselves as God loves us and view ourselves as God views us. Then we can overcome every insult, put-down, or hurt that comes against us, because we value ourselves, and see ourselves the way God values and sees us.

When Martin Luther was 10 years old, he and a friend went caroling house-to-house on Christmas Eve. At one house, a big man opened the door with a lamp in one hand and a club in the other hand. The two boys took off running with the man chasing them yelling, "Stop, stop!"

The boys finally took a wrong turn into a dead-end alley, and the man caught up with them. As he approached, they were quaking with fear. Only then did they realize that what they thought was a club was actually a big sausage this man was trying to share with them. Later on, Martin Luther said that he realized that all of his life he had been programmed to view God as someone with a big club, chasing after him saying, "Stop, stop!" In reality, God is a loving Father who is saying, "Stop...I want to give you the nourishment that you need."

How do you get over feelings of worthlessness? You must get in touch with the God of graciousness.

2. Feelings of failure. When we are young, we all set goals and have big dreams, then when we are around 40, it begins to dawn on us that we have not turned out the way we had planned.

David overcame his feelings of failure by realizing the providence of God. He said:

> *Where could I go to escape*
> *from you?*
> *Where could I get away from*
> *your presence?*
> *If I went up to heaven, you would*
> *be there;*
> *if I lay down in the world of the*
> *dead, you would be there.*
> *If I flew away beyond the east*

> *or lived in the farthest place in*
>   *the west,*
> *you would be there to lead me,*
>   *you would be there to help me.*
> *I could ask the darkness to*
>   *hide me*
>   *or the light around me to turn*
>   *into night,*
> *but even darkness is not dark*
>   *for you,*
>   *and the night is as bright as*
>   *the day.*
> *Darkness and light are the same*
>   *to you. (Psalm 139:7-12)*

Every time David encountered God, he found a God of goodness, One who provided his every need. The only way I know to overcome feelings of failure is to come to know a God who treasures you enough to constantly be with you, love you, and provide for you—and He always does!

Several years ago, I heard from a distant cousin whom I had never met. He said, "I understand you are researching the roots of the

Mann family."

I told him, "Yes, but they don't seem to go very far back. I keep finding information about robbers and thieves, but there doesn't seem to be much good."

He said, "Let me send you a letter written by your great grandmother." My great grandmother was Rosa Ward Mann, who married Andrew Jackson Mann right after the Civil War. He fought in two battles in the Civil War and was captured both times. After he left the service, he married Rosa, moved to Mississippi, and began farming. In 1874, while returning home with the proceeds of his crop, he was robbed and murdered. Rosa was only 18 years old when she was left pregnant, with two small children. She sold most of what she owned, put the rest in a wagon, and set out for Texas.

When she came to the Sabine River, it was a foggy day, and she broke an axle when she started up the riverbank on the Texas side. She suddenly saw a figure looming ahead of her in the mist and thought, "This is probably another robber like the one who murdered my husband."

But when the man approached her, he took her to his home and cared for her for several days while he fixed her wagon.

We have part of a letter Rosa wrote to a friend in Mississippi, in which she tells how she was hemorrhaging when she arrived in Texas, and she feared she would lose the baby. Later on, she had a healthy child and named him Carey Freeman Mann, my grandfather. My father was Carey Freeman Mann, Jr. The man who helped Rosa Ward, was Carey Freeman.

In the letter to her friend, Rosa wrote, "I will probably lose my baby. I may lose my life and my children. I could lose my faith if God were not so good."

How do you overcome feelings of failure? Get in touch with the providence of God. He is good, and He always provides exactly what we need, even if it is not in line with the dreams and plans we imagined for ourselves when we were young.

3. Feelings of obsolescence. Every day, as I view what is happening in the world of technology, I feel more and more obsolete. I could not turn on a computer if I wanted to, and until recently, I thought a mouse was something you exterminated. Now I know you don't poison it— you click it.

David has a marvelous portion in Psalm 139 that addresses this feeling of obsolescence. He said:

> *You created every part of me;*
> *you put me together in my mother's womb.*
> *I praise you because you are to be feared;*
> *all you do is strange and wonderful.*
> *I know it with all my heart.*
> *When my bones were being formed,*
> *carefully put together in my mother's womb,*
> *when I was growing there in secret,*
> *you knew that I was there—*
> *you saw me before I was born.*

> *The days allotted to me*
> *   had all been recorded in your*
> *   book,*
> *   before any of them ever began.*
> *O God, how difficult I find your*
> *   thoughts;*
> *   how many of them there are!*
> *If I counted them, they would be*
> *   more than the grains of sand.*
> *When I awake, I am still*
> *   with you. (Psalm 139:13-18)*

David overcame his feelings of being obsolete by getting in touch with a God who was still alive. Being obsolete is not only a state of mind; it is also a state of sin because the reality is that God has another chapter for all of us. The number one truth of our faith is that there is more to come. Our life does not end in death; death just closes one chapter. Every exit in the Kingdom of God is also an entrance to a new chapter.

You can begin after you are over the hill if you come to know God the way David describes Him in Psalm 139, as a God of grace and forgiveness, a God of providence, and a God of tomorrow.

CHAPTER FIVE

YOU CAN BEGIN AGAIN... AFTER BURNOUT

Burnout is the epidemic of the new century. In this time of unprecedented prosperity, we also have unprecedented breakdowns—people, in increasing numbers, who are unable to cope with the pace of life. I read the other day that more young people have ulcers in middle schools, than adults did 20 years ago. We are all caught up in a frenetic pace, and we tend to flame out quickly. Someone said, "We worship our work, play at our worship, and work at our play."

I am a veteran at burnout because I burned-out at the young age of 43. When I was 41 years old, I resigned a comfortable position and started a new church. I always had believed in working only a half-day—either the first 12 hours or the last 12 hours—but because I had a new church with only 60 members, and they could not adequately support my family and me, I also went into business. Soon, I was working another eight hours a day. Believing I could keep up the pace of 20-hour work days if I could just get in better shape, I began running five miles a day, instead of two miles a day. Then, at the age of 43, I had a heart attack, and was rushed into surgery for repair of a blocked artery. They later determined that my heart was actually squeezing the artery shut. When I woke up from surgery, I felt too sick to be in Heaven, and too cold to be in hell!

I started thinking, "Where in the Bible did someone burn out? Is there a Scriptural example, and if so, what did they do to recover?" I discovered that Moses is a classic example of beginning again after burnout. Moses was born at a turbulent time in Israel's history. Because the Pharaoh was killing all male Jewish babies in order to preserve Egypt's dominance over the Israelites, Moses was set adrift in a basket by his mother. He was rescued by Pharaoh's daughter, and grew up in the royal household nurtured by his own mother. As a young man, Moses witnessed the terrible suffering of his people. One day, after seeing an Egyptian slave driver kill an Israelite, he tried to get his people to rise up against their oppressors. After killing the Egyptian, Moses attempted to rally the Israelites, but no one would follow him. Moses then fled to the desert and remained there for 40 years.

It was there—in the desert, having burned-out from his own attempts to lead his people—that God resurrected him to a new life. You can read the story of Moses' meeting with God at the burning bush in Chapter 3 of the Book of Exodus. In this encounter, Moses learned three valuable lessons. When I applied these lessons to my life, they helped me recover from burnout. I trust they will do the same for you.

1. Moses discovered the power of solitude. Moses had never been alone in his life. He had never cultivated a private life of silence. Neither had I. I was very uncomfortable being alone. I constantly wanted people around me and a full schedule of things to do. On the rare occasions that I would "relax," I would work at something like hunting, fishing, or running. Everything I did was competitive. Sometimes, I would even try each day to see if I could pray ten minutes more than the day before. I rushed about here and there, and never developed an inward life of solitude and contemplation.

The Gospels reveal that Jesus guarded His solitude and time spent in prayer more than the time He would spend with His friends or with

His work. When one of His best friends—Lazarus—was dying, the family sent word for Jesus to come quickly and save him. Instead, Jesus went away by Himself for several days before responding.

If you lack a regular regimen of solitude, you cannot overcome burnout. Only in solitude did I realize I had never truly become acquainted with myself, and the more I got to know me, the less I liked me! However, by learning about myself and listening to God, I discovered that I was not all bad, and only then could I be comfortable being still, so that I could be contemplative.

2. Moses discovered the power of savoring. Savoring is finding something that you enjoy and prolonging it. When Moses saw the burning bush, he moved closer to see it. Only when God saw Moses coming closer did He call to him from the middle of the burning bush.

I have been to the Sinai Desert in August and burning bushes are not that rare due to spontaneous combustion caused by the intense heat. A burning bush was not uncommon, but the fact that it was not consumed was very unusual.

When God saw that Moses had the ability to really look at something with a sense of wonder and savor it, He spoke to him. God never speaks to us unless we slow down and take time to appreciate and savor.

When I was trying to recover from burnout, I underwent counseling, and one day I came home very upset. My wife, Lois, said to me, "I can help you if you would like some advice, but only if you ask me."

It took awhile, but I finally admitted to her that I was not recovering very well from my burnout. My life was still very crowded, and I was in control of nothing. I finally asked her what she thought I should do.

"You need to learn to savor things," she told me. "You gulp your food down, you work-out on a schedule—you do everything on a strict schedule. You need to slow down and learn to savor life."

My wife pointed out to me that even when I went hunting or fishing, I always had to hunt or fish to the limit. I did not really enjoy or savor what I was doing. Burnout comes from not being able to enjoy anything, even those things we supposedly love.

In my case, I finally learned to slow down so I could savor simple things—like going into my son's room and watching him while he slept. It is such a simple thing, but a treasure nonetheless. There is great power in savoring.

3. Moses discovered the power of surrendering. When God called Moses to deliver Israel, Moses argued with God that he could not do it— he had tried before and failed.

> *...the LORD asked him, "What are you holding?"*
>
> *"A walking stick," he answered.*
>
> *The LORD said, "Throw it on the ground." When Moses threw it down, it turned into a snake, and he ran away from it. Then the LORD said to Moses, "Reach down and pick it up by the tail." So Moses reached down and caught it, and it became a walking stick again. (Exodus 4:2-4)*

God was showing Moses that his previous cause had been righteous. Moses had wanted to set his people free, but with the wrong motivation. In *"Murder In The Cathedral,"* T.S. Eliot says, "The last temptation is the highest treason to do the right thing for the wrong reason." That was Moses' story. He had a righteous cause, but his motives were anger and vengeance, so he burned-out and went to hide in the desert for 40 years.

In my recovery from burnout, I discovered that I had brought all of the garbage from my childhood—the desires for achieving excellence and pleasing my father—into the ministry. I wanted to pastor the biggest church, to preach the greatest sermons, and to have more people attending Sunday school than anyone else. I never left the results to God. Even when I related to others, I wanted to save them, correct them, and tell them what they should believe.

I finally learned that I had to stop trying to be in charge, and I had to accept and enjoy people, regardless of who they are or what they do. It was a liberating moment in my life when I realized that God did not need my help! Burnout is actually an overestimation of the scope of your ability to change the world.

Like Moses, and like me, you can begin again after burnout by discovering the power of solitude, the power of savoring, and the power of surrender.

CHAPTER SIX

YOU CAN BEGIN AGAIN... AFTER BETRAYAL

When I was in the fourth grade, I sang in the choir, and one day someone wrote an obscene note on the back of my songbook. Someone else saw it and reported it, and I was called to the principal's office. The school crossing guard was there in his police-like uniform, and he told me, "It is bad boys like you that end up in reform school!"

I had no idea who wrote the obscenity on my book, but everyone kept browbeating me and interrogating me. Finally, they made me stand in front of an assembly of all the students and apologize for something I had not done. That single event launched a two-year period during which I was an absolute hellion at school. At one point, I even tried to burn the school down!

One day, one of the coaches who felt I had some athletic promise, asked me, "When are you going to stop treating yourself as badly as they treated you?" That was a turning point in my young life. I realized that I could spend the remainder of my life grieving over that incident, or I could put it behind me.

If you have yet to be wronged or betrayed,

just wait, you will be! Everyone, at sometime in life, is betrayed or wronged by someone they love. The question is, how do you begin again after betrayal?

Joseph is a classic, Biblical model of how to begin again after betrayal. Joseph was the eleventh son of Jacob. His father gave him a beautiful coat of many colors, signifying the special place Joseph occupied in his father's heart. When Joseph shared his dreams of his brothers being subservient to him, they became enraged, threw him into a pit, and later sold him to a passing caravan of Egyptians. In Egypt, Joseph became the head servant in the house of a military officer named Potiphar. When Potiphar's wife tried to seduce him and Joseph rejected her advances, she became angry. Then, she falsely accused him, and had him imprisoned.

Through his ability to interpret dreams, Joseph became a trusted advisor to Pharoah, and was placed second in command in the nation of Egypt. During a severe famine, Joseph's brothers came to Egypt to secure food. Joseph eventually revealed his identity to them, they were reconciled, and he moved his father, Jacob, and the entire family to Egypt.

Later on, when Jacob died, Joseph's brothers became concerned:

> *After the death of their father, Joseph's brothers said, "What if Joseph still hates us and plans to pay us back for all the harm we did to him?" So they sent a message to Joseph: "Before our father died, he told us to ask you, 'Please forgive the crime your brothers committed when they wronged you.' Now please forgive us the wrong that we, the servants of your father's God, have done." Joseph cried when he received this message.*
>
> *Then his brothers themselves came and bowed down before him. "Here we are before you as your slaves," they said.*
>
> *But Joseph said to them, "Don't be afraid; I can't put myself in the place of God. You plotted evil against me, but God turned it into good, in order to pre-*

serve the lives of many people who are alive today because of what happened. You have nothing to fear. I will take care of you and your children." So he reassured them with kind words that touched their hearts. (Genesis 50:15-21)

In this passage, there are three clues that reveal how Joseph was able to begin again after betrayal.

1. Joseph practiced good grief. There are two kinds of grief. First, there is destructive grief, where you allow what has happened to you to make you bitter. You dwell and fixate on it; you nourish anger and resentment all of your life, and you continually live in the past.

Then there is a second type of grief, which Joseph practiced. I call it "good grief," the kind of grief that moves you forward and makes you *better,* instead of *bitter.* When Joseph received the message from his brothers, he wept. He knew how to release his grief. Jesus said, "Blessed are those who mourn"—those who know how to grieve positively so they can move from their hurts to triumph. That is good grief.

About 12 years ago, one of our daughters was on drugs and living a wayward lifestyle. About once a month I would come home to find that my wife, Lois, had been crying all day. Being the control-freak that I am, I always want to fix everything, so I would tell her, "You can't continue doing this. It is unhealthy."

Lois would always say, "Wait just a minute! That is my monthly emotional bath. You've had burnout, heart surgery, and four sinus surgeries. You'll continue to have surgeries, and I'll continue to cry!" She was grieving positively. I was the one grieving negatively.

At every hurt, we have two choices—to let them make us bitter, or better. Joseph wept and forgave. He chose to grieve positively.

2. Joseph practiced miraculous mercy. Often when we are hurt, we practice a false kind of mercy. We manipulate—we forgive someone a wrong, but then remind him or her of it every day, emphasizing how big we are for forgiving. That is not true forgiveness, nor is it true mercy.

Joseph practiced miraculous mercy, the kind

that changes people's lives. He said, "I'm not God!" He embraced his brothers, and when they heard his words, their hearts melted.

I often ask preachers, "Why do you accuse, threaten, and tell people they are lost and going to hell?" The Apostle Paul said that it is God's mercy that leads people to change. I would want no one to change simply out of fear of being struck down by God. The only people I have seen change in a healthy way are those who come to experience the unconditional forgiveness and mercy of God. Like Joseph, we need to look beyond our wounds and practice miraculous mercy.

In his book, *"Forgive & Forget; Healing the Hurts We Don't Deserve,"* Louis Smedes tells a fable which draws a distinction between healthy and unhealthy mercy.

In this story, set in the village of Faking in Innermost Freezeland, there lived a long, slim baker named Frederic. He was so upright that he seemed to spew righteousness from his thin, thin lips. As a result, the people of the village preferred to stay away from him.

Frederic's wife, Hilda, was the opposite of Frederic. She was short, rotund, and open-hearted. She seemed to invite everyone to come close to her, so that they could share her cheer and warmth. Hilda respected her self-righteous husband, and she loved him as much as he would allow her. But her heart ached for something more than his righteousness, and therein was planted the seed of a great sadness.

One morning, after kneading his dough, Frederic came home to find a stranger in his bed lying on Hilda's bosom. News of her adultery soon became the talk of the village. "Surely," everybody said, "Frederic would cast her out," so righteous was he. But he surprised everyone by forgiving her because the Good Book demanded that he do so. But in his heart of hearts, he could never forgive her for bringing shame on his righteous house. He could only pretend to forgive her. Whenever he thought about her, he despised her as if she were a common tramp.

But his fakery did not set well in Heaven, for each time he felt his secret hatred for her, an angel would come down and drop a pebble in his heart. As the pebbles multiplied and multiplied, Frederic's heart became so heavy that the top half of his body began to bend forward as he walked. Finally, he wished he was dead, and he called on God to help him.

The angel came back and informed him that he could be saved only by the miracle of the magic eyes. He would have to look back to the beginning of his hurt and see Hilda not as a wicked person, but as a weak person who needed him.

"How do I get the miracle of the magic eyes?" he asked the angel.

The angel said, "Only ask, desiring as you ask, and you will receive them, and every time you see Hilda with your new eyes, a pebble will be lifted from your heart."

At first, Frederic couldn't ask for the magic eyes because he had grown to love his hatred too much. But finally, his heavy heart drove him to ask, and each time he did, his heart grew lighter. Soon Hilda began to change before his very eyes, wonderfully and mysteriously. He now saw her as a woman who loved him, instead of as a traitor. Now, he walked much straighter, and his lips even began to look a little fuller. He invited Hilda back into his heart again, and together they began a journey into their second season of humble joy.

I love this story because it shows the difference between manipulating mercy, and the kind of mercy that changes peoples' lives. You can begin again after you have been betrayed if you will practice miraculous mercy.

3. Joseph practiced healthy hope. Just as there are two kinds of mercy, there are also two kinds of hope. There is a negative, unhealthy hope that makes us think we can right all the wrongs done to us. Then there is a healthy hope that tries to see a hurt as an opportunity to grow and fulfill God's destiny for our lives.

Joseph is a great example of this kind of hope—healthy hope. He said to his brothers, *"You plotted evil against me, but God turned it into good..."* (Genesis 50:20) Healthy hope is viewing our hurt in a larger context—as a part of God's plan.

You can begin again after betrayal if you

YOU CAN BEGIN AGAIN

learn to hope in a healthy way and see God's hand in all things. The Bible does not say that all things are good. It says that God is in all things working His good (Romans 8:28). When you are betrayed, do not continually ask, "Why me, God?" Instead, begin to ask, "Why have I been given this experience?" God is at work in everything that happens to us, and even though we may not understand our present suffering, He always provides for us according to His plan. Joseph asked the big question and was able to get past his hurt. As we now know, he went on to save multitudes.

You can begin again after you have been betrayed if you practice good grief, miraculous mercy, and healthy hope. You have a choice to use your hurt and betrayal for triumph or tragedy.

In closing, let me emphasize that beginning again is impossible unless you have had a spiritual awakening and have come to know God in a personal way. My sincere prayer is that you come to know Jesus Christ as your Savior, because through His grace, you can begin again!

ABOUT THE AUTHOR

Dr. Gerald Mann is the senior pastor of Riverbend Church in Austin, Texas. He has three children and four grandchildren. His weekly television program, **Real Life!** is now available in over 70 million homes. He is the author of numerous books, including *Common Sense Religion, When One Day at a Time Is Too Long,* and *The Book of Wisecracks.*

NOTES

NOTES

NOTES

NOTES